FANATICISM,

AND ITS RESULTS:

OR,

FACTS VERSUS FANCIES.

BY A SOUTHERNER.

BALTIMORE:
PRINTED BY JOSEPH ROBINSON.
1860.

TO

THE HONORABLE HENRY A. WISE,

The True-Hearted Virginia Gentleman,

The Patriot, the Statesman,

AND

THE TRUE AND UNDAUNTED

Defender

OF

Southern Rights

AND

Southern Institutions,

THIS BOOK

IS

Respectfully and Gratefully

DEDICATED

BY

A SOUTHERNER.

FANATICISM, AND ITS RESULTS:

OR

FACTS VERSUS FANCIES.

In offering to the public the few imperfect and hastily written thoughts which are herein contained, we have been influenced by no party zeal, or sectional motives. The only feelings which have influenced us, have been truth and justice. A desire to do justice to both parties—North and South. To point out who are in truth the enemies of the Union—to warn the friends of the Union of the danger which threatens it—to point out how it can be met—and we beg leave to express the hope, that it may by this course be averted. We love the Union as our fathers made it, and we earnestly trust that it may continue, a union of free and equal sovereign States.

The present period of its existence is one of deep interest to every citizen of America; indeed, we may say to the whole world—the eyes of all the world are turned to us. The voice of warning is heard in every part of our land. Our national existence is threatened by a power far more terrible than ever sacked the "Eternal City," or swept like a blighting storm over the civilized world. Treason is at work amongst us. The voice of discord has been heard even in the walls of our National Senate house. The voice of Washington bidding his countrymen "frown indignantly upon the first dawning of an attempt to alienate one portion of the country from the other, or to sever the political bonds which connect its various parts," is unheard amidst the din of excited sectional passions and party strife. Disunion—a word which (used as it is,) should cause the blush of shame to mantle the cheek of every true American, has been thundered in our ears by an excited sectional party. There are clouds in the sky—dark and terrific storms are brewing—already the lurid flashes of their lightnings have been seen, and the deep mutterings of their thunders have been heard. God only knows how soon they will burst upon us in all their awful fury. And then—but the heart sickens at the thought of what must follow. We cannot trace it. We will for the present drop the curtain over the dark picture which has been presented to our view. We shall be called upon soon enough to lift it. But the questions arise: What has brought about such terrible results in this great and enlightened country? What demon of anarchy has entered into our midst? What is it that is so fraught with danger to the Union? Fearlessly and unhesitatingly we give but one answer to all of these questions. The words are simple, but they are full of meaning and power.—Our answer is:

THE DEMON OF ABOLITIONISM.

We would not do injustice to any one, or any party, and we trust that we will be able to show that our assertion is true, and that the only traitors in the land are those who are known as the Abolition and Republican parties.

These parties are professedly two separate and distinct organizations, but as we consider them the same in all but the name, we shall, hereafter, in speaking of them, use only the words "*Abolitionists*," and "*the North*." We wish to be distinctly understood, that, in speaking of the North as false to the Union, we mean only that portion known as the "Abolitionists." We know that there are many strong national and conservative men at the North. We know that pure and untarnished patriotism exists there; but alas! it is in an almost hopeless minority. We propose giving a hasty sketch of the Abolition party, and their acts; and, in doing so, we shall confine ourselves strictly to the record that History has given us.

It is well-known that there has always existed in the Union, ever since its foundation, a strong feeling of enmity towards Slavery.

The first public act of this party, that we can find recorded, is a Memorial presented in the House of Representatives, in Congress, on the 12th of February, 1790. We copy it from Messrs. Gales and Seaton's Congressional Debates. We give it entire, because it is one of the most interesting ever offered, and embodies the spirit of a majority of the rest.

"*A Memorial of the Pennsylvania Society for Promoting the Abolition of Slavery, the Relief of Free Negroes unlawfully held in bondage, and the improvement of the African race.*

"The Memorial respectfully showeth: That, from a regard for the happiness of mankind, an association was formed several years since, in this State, by a number of her citizens, of various religious denominations, for promoting the Abolition of Slavery, and for the relief of those unlawfully held in bondage. A just and acute conception of the true principles of liberty, as it is spread through the land, produced accessions to their numbers; many friends to their cause, and a legislative co-operation with their views, which, by the blessing of Divine Providence, have been successfully directed to the relieving from bondage a large number of their fellow-creatures of the African race. They have also the satisfaction to observe that, in consequence of that spirit of philanthropy, and genuine liberty, which is generally diffusing its beneficial influence, similar institutions are forming at home and abroad.

"That mankind are all formed by the same Almighty Being, alike objects of His care, and equally designed for the enjoyment of happiness, the Christian religion teaches us to believe, and the political creed of America fully coincides with the position.

"Your memorialists, particularly engaged in attending to the distresses arising from Slavery, believe it to be their indispensable duty to present this subject to your notice. They have observed with real satisfaction, that many important and salutary powers are vested in you 'for promoting the welfare, and securing the blessings of liberty to the people of the United States;' and as they conceive that these blessings ought rightfully to be administered, without distinction of color, to all descriptions of people, so they indulge themselves in the pleasing expectation, that nothing which can be done for the relief of the unhappy objects of their care, will be either omitted or delayed.

"From a persuasion that equal liberty was originally the portion, and is still birthright of all men, and influenced by the strong ties of humanity, and the principles of their institutions, your memorialists consider themselves bound to use all justifiable endeavors to loosen the bonds of Slavery, and promote a general enjoyment of the blessings of freedom.

"Under these impressions, they earnestly entreat your serious attention to the subject of Slavery; that you will be pleased to countenance the restoration of liberty to those unhappy men, who alone in this land of freedom, are degraded into perpetual bondage, and who, amidst the general joy of surrounding freemen, are groaning in servile subjection; that you will devise means for removing this inconsistency from the character of the American people; that you will promote mercy and justice towards this distressed race; and that you will step to the very verge of the power vested in you, for discouraging every species of traffic in the persons of our fellow-men.

BENJAMIN FRANKLIN,
President.

PHILADELPHIA, *February* 3, 1790."

After a warm debate, all the memorials which had been presented during the session, were referred to a Select Committee.

This Committee, in due time, offered its report, which was referred to the Committee of the whole House; which, after amending the report of the Select Committee, adopted the following resolution:

"That Congress have no authority to interfere in the emancipation of Slaves, or in the treatment of them, within any of the States; it remaining with the several States alone to provide any regulations therein which humanity and true policy may require."

On the 26th of November, a petition was presented from Warner Mifflin, a Quaker, in relation to the Slave Trade, and to the treatment of Slaves in the United States. It was laid on the table. Two days after, on motion of Mr. Steele, of N. C., it was returned to him by the Clerk.

January 30th, 1797, Mr. Swanwick, of Pa., presented a petition of four Slaves, representing that they had been emancipated, but under some law of N. Carolina they could be again reduced to Slavery; that to avoid this they had escaped to Pennsylvania, after suffering many hardships, praying Congress to look into the case. Also into that of another Negro who had been emancipated, again reduced to Slavery, and had escaped; but under the Fugitive Slave Law, he had been arrested and confined in jail. Congress, by a vote of yeas 33, nays 50, refused to receive the petition, stating that they had no right to interfere with the laws of any State.

On the 30th of November, 1797, Mr. Gallatin, of Pa., presented a memorial from the Quakers of Pennsylvania, calling attention to the condition of the Slaves, and also protesting against all kinds of vicious and expensive amusements. After a long debate on the reception of the petition, it was referred to a Select Committee of five.

Jan. 29th, 1798, Mr. Sitgreaves, of Penn., the Chairman of the Committee, reported "that the facts referred to were exclusively of judicial cognizance; that therefore it is not competent for the Legislature to do any thing in the business." The report concluded by recommending "that the memorialists be allowed to withdraw their petition." Feb. 14th, 1798, the House adopted the report of the Committee. The same petition was offered in the Senate, but was afterwards withdrawn.

June 21st, 1805, Mr. Logan, of Pa., pesented to the Senate a petition from the Quakers, praying Congress to adopt some means to prevent the introduction of Slavery into the Territories. It was received by a vote of yeas 19, nays 9. A similar petition was presented and referred in the House the same day.

January, 1817, a number of petitions were presented against the Slave Trade between the Middle and Southern States—they were read and referred.

During the first session of the 16th Congress, numerous petitions were received, asking the prohibition of Slavery in all the States hereafter to be admitted into the Union. Some were referred, others merely read.

On the 12th of February, 1827, Mr. Barney, of Baltimore, presented to the House a memorial signed by certain citizens of Baltimore, praying Congress to pass a law providing that all children hereafter born of Slave parents in the District of Columbia, shall be free after a certain age. He moved that it be printed. After a debate, the motion to print was lost.

December 12th, 1831, Mr. John Quincy Adams presented 15 petitions from numerous inhabitants of Pennsylvania, praying for the abolition of Slavery in the district of Columbia. They were referred to the Committee on the District of Columbia.

On December the 19th, that Committee made their report, asking to be discharged from further consideration of such parts of the petitions before them as asked the abolishment of Slavery in the District of Columbia.

In the Senate, January 7th, 1836, Mr. Morris, of Ohio, presented several petitions from citizens of Ohio, (one of which was signed by ladies,) asking the abolition of Slavery in the District of Columbia. He moved to refer them to the Committee on the District of Columbia.

January 11th, Mr. Buchanan presented a petition from the Quakers. He moved that it be read and its prayer rejected.

A long debate ensued upon the reception of these two petitions. During this debate; on the 28th of January, 1836, Mr. Swift, of Vermont, presented another petition to the same effect, from the citizens of Vermont; he requested that it might be read. A debate ensued upon its reception. On motion of Mr. Buchanan, the petitions were laid on the table, to be called up when the Senate was ready to make a final disposition of them.

March 9th, 1836, the question was brought up, on the motion to receive the petition presented by Mr. Buchanan, and it was decided to receive the petition.

March 11th, 1836, the motion of Mr. Buchanan to reject the petition, passed the Senate, by a vote—yeas 34, nays 6.

During the first Session of the Twenty-fourth Congress, Abolition petitions were literally rained upon the House. They gave rise to a variety of resolutions relative to the powers of Congress over the subject, and the proper disposition that should be made of them.

On the 8th of February, 1836, Mr. H. L. Pinckney, of S. C., having obtained a suspension of the rules, offered the following resolution:

"*Resolved*, That all memorials which have been offered, or may hereafter be presented to this House, praying for the abolition of Slavery in the District of Columbia, and also the resolutions offered by an honorable member from Maine, (Mr. Jarvis,) with the amendment thereto proposed by an honorable member of Virginia, (Mr. Wise,) and every other paper or proposition that may be submitted in relation to the subject, be referred to a select committee, with instructions to report, that Congress possesses no Constitutional authority to interfere in any way with the institutions of Slavery in any of the States of this Confederacy; and that, in the opinion of this House, Congress ought not to interfere in any way with Slavery in the District of Columbia, because it would be a violation of the public faith, unwise, impolitic, and dangerous to the Union, assigning such reasons for these conclusions as in the judgment of the committee may be best calculated to enlighten the public mind, to repress agitation, to allay excitement, to sustain and preserve the just rights of the Slave-Holding States, and of the people of this District, and to re-establish harmony and tranquillity among the the various sections of the Union."

This resolution was adopted, and the committee appointed.

On the 18th of May, 1836, Mr. Pinckney presented the report of the Committee. We give only the concluding resolutions;

"*Resolved*, That Congress possesses no constitutional authority to interfere in any way with the institution of Slavery in any of the States of this Confederacy.

"*Resolved*, That Congress ought not to interfere in any way with Slavery in the District of Columbia.

"And whereas, it is extremely important and desirable that the agitation of this subject should be finally arrested, for the purpose of restoring tranquillity to the public mind, your Committee respectfully recommend the adoption of the following resolution:

"*Resolved*, that all Petitions, memorials, resolutions, propositions or papers, relating in any way, or to any extent whatever, to the subject of Slavery, or the abolition of Slavery, shall, without being either printed or referred, be laid upon the table, and that no further action whatever shall be had thereon."

May 25th, 1836, the first resolution was adopted by a vote of yeas 182, nays 9. The second resolution was adopted by a vote of yeas 132, nays 45. The third resolution passed by a vote of yeas 117, nays 68.

The Senate, during the second session of the 25th Congress, invariably pursued the plan of laying the question of the reception of abolition petitions on the table.

December 27th, 1837, Mr. Calhoun offered to the Senate the following series of resolutions, which have become as famous as his name, and which will be read with pleasure by all.

"1. *Resolved*, That in the adoption of the Federal Constitution, the States adopting the same, acted, severally, as free, independent, and sovereign States, and that each for itself, by its own voluntary assent, entered the Union with a view to its increased security against all dangers, domestic as well as foreign, and the more perfect and secure enjoyment of its advantages, natural, political and social.

"2. *Resolved*, That in delegating a portion of their powers to be exercised by the Federal Government, the States retained, severally, the exclusive and sole right over their own domestic institutions and police, and are alone responsible for them; and that any intermeddling of one or more States, or a combination of their citizens, with the domestic institutions and police of the others, on any ground, or under any pretext whatever, political, moral or religious, with a view to their alteration or subversion, is an assumption of superiority not warranted by the Constitution, insulting to the States interfered with, tending to endanger their domestic peace and tranquillity, subversive to the objects for which the Constitution was formed, and by necessary consequence, tending to weaken and destroy the Union itself.

"3. *Resolved*, That this government was instituted and adopted by the several States of this Union, as a common agent, in order to carry into effect the power which they had delegated by the Constitution, for their mutual security and prosperity; and that, in fulfilment of this high and sacred trust, this government is bound so to exercise its powers as to give, as far as may be practicable, increased stability and security to the domestic institutions of the States that compose the Union, and that it is the solemn duty of the Government to resist all attempts by one portion of the Union, to use it as an instrument to attack the domestic institutions of another, or to weaken or destroy such institutions.

"4. *Resolved*, That domestic Slavery as it exists in the Southern and Western States of this Union, composes an important part of their domestic institutions, inherited from their ancestors, and existing at the adoption of the Constitution, by which it is recognized as constituting an essential element in the distribution of its powers among the States, and that no change of opinion or feeling on the part of the other States of the Union, in relation to it, can justify them or their citizens, in open and systematic attacks thereon, with the view to its overthrow; and that all such attacks are in manifest violation of the mutual and solemn pledge to protect and defend each other, given by the States respectively, on entering into the Constitutional compact, which formed the Union, and as such, is a manifest breach of faith, and a violation of the most solemn obligations.

(As originally offered.)

"5th. *Resolved*, That the intermeddling of any State or States, or their citizens to abolish Slavery in this District, or in any of the Territories, on the ground, or under the pretext, that it is immoral or sinful, or the passage of any act or measure of Congress with that view, would be a direct and dangerous attack on the institutions of all the Slaveholding States.

(As amended by Mr. Clay, of Ky.)

"5th. *Resolved*, That when the District of Columbia was ceded by the States of Maryland and Virginia, to the United States, domestic Slavery existed in both of those States, including the ceded territory; and that, as it still continues in both of them, it could not be abolished within the District, without a violation of that good faith which was implied in the cession, and in the acceptance of the territory, nor unless compensation were offered for the Slaves, without a manifest infringement of an amendment of the Constitution of the United States; nor without exciting a degree of just alarm and apprehension in the States recognizing Slavery, far transcending in mischievous tendency any possible benefit which could be accomplished by the Abolition.

"*And Resolved*, That any attempt of Congress to abolish Slavery in any Territory of the United States in which it exists, would create serious alarm, and just apprehension in the States sustaining that domestic institution; would be a violation of good faith towards the inhabitants of such Territory who have been permitted to settle with, and hold Slaves, because the people of such Territory have not asked for the abolition of Slavery therein, and because, that, when any such Territory shall be admitted into the Union as a State, the people thereof will be entitled to decide that question for themselves."

Mr. Morris, of Ohio, moved to strike out the words "moral and religious" in the first resolution. His motion was lost.

The first resolution was adopted by a vote of yeas 31, nays 13.

Only 9 votes were cast against the second resolution.

The third resolution was adopted by a a vote of yeas 31, nays 11.

The fourth resolution was adopted by a vote of yeas 34, nays 5.

The vote on the 5th resolution, as amended by Mr. Clay, was as follows: yeas 36, nays 8.

The final resolution of Mr. Clay was adopted by a vote of yeas 35, nays 9.

During the same Session of Congress, the excitement in the House caused by these abolition petitions was intense. For a description of it, we refer our readers to the able account given by Col. Thomas H. Benton, in his "Thirty Years View."

We would gladly insert a portion of it, but our limits will not allow us to do so.

In 1821, the Missouri Compromise Bill was passed. Our readers are too familiar with the history of this celebrated peace-offering from the South to the Demon of Abolitionism, to render it necessary for us to enter into any history of it.

The Senate, during the Second Session of the Twenty-Fourth Congress, continued to receive numerous abolition petitions; all motions to receive them were invariably laid on the table. The Senate has pursued this course up to the present day. During the Twenty-Fourth and Twenty-Fifth Congresses, the House concluded to lay all abolition petitions on the table, without being either printed or referred.

January 28th, 1840, the amendment of Mr. W. Cost Johnson, to an amendment offered by Mr. John Quincy Adams, to the rules, was adopted under the title of the 21st rule. The Hon. W. Smith, of Va., in his eloquent and able speech, delivered in Congress in December, 1859, gives an interesting history of this rule. To it we refer our readers. The rule was as follows:

"That no petition, memorial or resolution, or other paper, praying the abolition of Slavery in the District of Columbia, or any State or Territory, or the Slave trade between the States or Territories of the United States, in which it now exists, shall be received by this House, or entertained in any way whatever."

The adoption was by a vote of yeas 114, nays 108.

This 21st rule was rescinded on motion of Mr. John Quincy Adams, on the 3d of December, 1844, by a vote of yeas 108, nays 80.

December 1st, 1845. Mr. Chapman, of Ala., made a motion to revive it; but it was lost by a vote of yeas 84, nays 121.

February 25th, 1850, Mr. Giddings, of Ohio, in the House, presented two petitions; one from certain citizens of Pennsylvania, and the other from certain citizens of Delaware. They were as follows:

"We, the undersigned, inhabitants of Pennsylvania and Delaware, believing that the Federal Constitution, in pledging the strength of the whole nation to support Slavery, violates the Divine law, makes war upon human rights, and is grossly inconsistent with Republican principles; that its attempt to unite Slavery in one body politic, has brought upon the country, great and manifold evils, and has fully proved that no such Union can exist but by the sacrifice of freedom to the supremacy of Slavery, respectfully ask you to propose and devise, without delay, some plan for the immediate and peaceful dissolution of the American Union."

Mr. Giddings asked that these resolutions might be referred to a Select Committee, who should be instructed to enquire:

"*First.*—Whether disaffection with our Federal Union exists among the people of these States?

"*Secondly.*—If so, to what extent does such discontent exist?

"*Thirdly.*—From what has such disaffection arisen?

"*Fourthly.*—The proper means of restoring confidence among the people?"

It was decided by a vote of yeas 8, nays 162, not to receive these petitions.

Those who voted affirmatively, were Messrs. Allen, of Mass.; Durkee, of Wisconsin; Giddings, of Ohio; Goodenow, of Me.; Howe, of Pa.; Julian, of Indiana; Preston King, of N. Y.; and Root, of Ohio. We wish all to know them.

Feb. 1st, 1850, the same petitions were offered in the Senate by Mr. Hale, of N. H.

Mr. Webster suggested that such a preamble as the following should have been prefixed to the petition:

"Gentlemen, members of Congress: Whereas, at the commencement of the Session, you, and each of you, took your solemn oaths in the presence of God and on the Holy Evangelists, that you would support the Constitution of the U. States, now. therefore, we pray you to take immediate steps to break up the Union and overthrow the Constitution of the United States, as soon as you can. And as in duty bound, we will ever pray."

Senators CHASE, HALE and SEWARD, were all that voted for it.

Other petitions have since been presented, but we will not weary our readers by recording them here.

The efforts of the Abolitionists soon brought about the terrible crisis of 1850, which is too well known to our readers to require any explanation from us; and from which the Union was only rescued by the superhuman efforts of Henry Clay.

Such, then, is a brief and hasty sketch of their acts in Congress. Much of it we have been compelled to pass over hastily. All that we have here reported, can be found in the "Annals of Congress," from which our information has been gained.

We propose now to glance hastily at some of their acts, during their existence, as one of the great political parties of the country.

It made its first appearance as such, in 1840, with the following ticket: "For President, James G. Birney, of Michigan; for Vice-President, Francis J. Lemoyne, of Pennsylvania." During this campaign, this party polled 7.000 votes. In 1844, they again offered Mr. Birney as their candidate for the Presidency, and polled 62,140 votes.

In 1844, Martin Van Buren was their candidate for the Presidency, having been nominated in convention at Buffalo. This convention adopted the first abolition platform that we can find; and in it, was announced the stern and unyielding determination of the party to root out Slavery by every constitutional means in their power. The more ultra Anti-Slavery men supported Gerrit Smith, and the vote polled by the entire party was 296,232.

In 1852, John P. Hale was its nominee, and he polled 157,296 votes.

John C. Fremont, in 1856, received the support of the entire Abolition party, and the number of votes polled amounted to 1,341,812.

The same Convention which nominated Fremont, adopted the Republican platform, from which we give the following:

"Resolved, * * * *That we deny the authority of Congress, of a territorial legislature, or any individual or association of individuals, to give legal existence to Slavery in any Territory of the United States, while the present Constitution shall be maintained.*"

Such, then, is an outline of the History of this Abolition party. A party which has increased with the most surprising rapidity. And how has this been done? By appeals addressed to the worst feelings, and most ungovernable passions of mankind. By poisoning their hearts with tales of Negro wrongs and sufferings, by base and vile slanders upon their brethren of the South. By a rapid review of the brief sketch of the party that we have given, we find:

First.—That the Abolition party was the first to agitate the Slavery question.

Second.—That in spite of the assertions of Congress, that it had no right to interfere with "the domestic institutions and police" of the States—in spite of the assertions of Congress, that it would be "unwise, impolitic, a violation of good faith," towards the Slave-holding States—in spite of their warnings that this continued agitation was fraught with imminent danger to the South, we find them persisting in their mad and unreasonable course, regardless alike of warning and entreaty.

Third.—We find them by their course, causing all the great and terrible crises from which the country has been rescued by the great triumvirate—Clay, Calhoun, and Webster.

Fourth.—We find that their whole course has been one of aggression upon Southern rights and institutions.

Lastly, we find that, not satisfied with their mad and unconstitutional career, they were the first and the only party to petition for the Dissolution of the Union. Such are the causes of the present unfortunate condition of the Union. We have asserted that the danger which now threatens the Union was caused by "the Demon of Abolitionism." We have given their own acts as proofs of this assertion, and we leave it, appealing to all fair and candid persons if we have not fully maintained our position. Having shown, as we believe, that the North has been the cause of all of our sectional discord, let us see what has been the conduct of the South from the beginning of the Slavery agitation, up to the present day.

By a reference to "the Annals of Congress," we shall find that not a single voice of discord or threatening, up to the period of, and after the Missouri Compromise, was heard from the South. Nothing but expostulation and entreaty was heard from her. In eloquent terms did her sons point out to their brethren of the North the danger and the folly of their course. Earnestly did they entreat them to cease the agitation of a question which could do no good, and which was becoming so dangerous to the welfare and prosperity of the Union. Sacrifices they did make, and have ever made. They asked no sacrifice from the North—they made no unreasonable demands. All that they asked was, that the North should abide by its compact with them—that it should cease to aggress them.

"The Slave-Holding States have done no wrong to their Free-State sisters. Virginia, in her generosity and nobleness of soul, gave five great States to freedom, as it is called, and to the Union. Her great Captain gave us liberty, and her Captains at the head of the Armies of the Union, ever led them on to victory. Her Sages have piloted the Ship of State through every trial. They have kept their looms in motion. To them they can trace their great wealth, and the luxurious embellishment of their barren country" The South has ever said to the North, "Rear up your palatial residences; make your country 'to smile and blossom as the rose;' let your halls of science be filled with your aspiring youth; let your proud Navies stretch their wings to every breeze and over every sea; we are content; may we share in the pride and glory of your prosperity. *We ask no return, but to be left in peace—to the enjoyment of our rights—to be let alone. This is all that we have ever asked; it is all that we ask now.*"

For the sake of the Union—under the spell of the glory and greatness which she has given to that Union—hallowed as it is to her by the thousand fond memories connected with it, the South has always submitted to insult and oppression from the North, because she has had but one aim in view—the perpetuation of the Union. She has gone farther, she has met these insults and agressions not with blows or resentful words, but with sacrifices of her constitutional rights, with compromises until she has now nothing left to sacrifice, to compromise, but her homes and her honor.

Every one who has studied the subject, knows that the Missouri Compromise was unconstitutional. Mr. Clay himself avowed this. But, as the North would be satisfied with nothing else, the South consented to it, because she was willing to make any sacrifice to preserve the Union.

It is not our intention to discuss the Slavery question in this article. We simply wish to give a history of the troubles which have agitated the country for such a long time, to show the true position of both sections of the country. To defend the South against the unjust accusations which are being hurled at it, and to give our views as to how the South should act under the present circumstances, and how the danger may be averted.

We have said that the North has been the quarter from which the dangerous sentiments of *disunion* have been heard. The South has been charged with "*fire-eating*,"—"*disunionism.*" This charge we pronounce false. But first, let us see what additional proofs we can offer in support of our assertion, that the spirit of disunion has been fostered, and has shown itself in the North, and that it is from that section that the danger which now threatens the Union has burst upon us.

We have already shown that the Slavery agitation was begun and fostered at the North—that the only prayers to Congress for dissolution came from the North, and we now intend to show that this spirit of disunion has been fostered and advocated by the Northern Pulpit, Press, Bar, and Legislatures, as well as by their Representatives in Congress. That they have been the means of spreading treason and discord in our midst.

But to begin:

The New York National Anti-Slavery Standard, of June 21, 1856, says: "The North is in a state of excitement, temporary, perhaps, but real for the time; and the widening lines of division between North and South are growing deep and distinct." It then goes on to rejoice in the growing alienation of the North from the South, and counsels resistance to everything like Slavery. Yes, even though the rights of the South are secured to her by Constitional enactments—by the Constitution itself—this paper counsels resistance to them—resistance to the Constitution, and consequently to the Federal Government itself; or, in other words, *it advocates treason*.

The Rev. Henry Ward Beecher, at a meeting held in his church, to promote emigration to Kansas, said:

"He believed that the Sharpe rifle was a truly moral agency, and there was orem moral power in one of those instruments, so far as the Slave-Holders of Kansas were concerned, than in a thousand Bibles. You might just as well, said he, read the Bible to buffaloes, as to those fellows who follow Atchison and Stringfellow; but they have a supreme respect for the logic that is embodied in Sharpe's rifles. The Bible is addressed to the conscience; but when you address it to them, it has no effect—there is no conscience there. Though he was a peace-man, he had the greatest regard for Sharpe's rifles, and the pluck that induced those New England men to use them. In such issues, under such circumstances, he was decidedly in favor of such instrumentalities. General Scott had said that it was difficult to get the New England men into a quarrel, but when they are waked up, and have the law on their side, they are the ugliest customers in the world."

When we see the pulpit used to excite the worst passions of mankind—to arm men against their brothers' lives—when we hear the Bible placed beneath Sharpe's rifles, by one who calls himself a minister of God—when we hear murder defended and advocated by the clergy, what can we expect from the laity? But we have no desire to dwell upon this article—it carries its comment with it. It is nothing more than we expected from such a man.

Mr. W. O. Duval, a prominent Abolitionist, says:

"I sincerely hope a civil war may soon burst upon the country. I want to see American Slavery abolished in my time. Then, my fervent prayer is, that England, France and Spain, may take this Slavery-accursed nation into their special consideration; and when the time arrives for the streets of the cities of this 'land of the free and home of the brave,' to run with blood to the horses' bridles, if the writer of this be living, there will be one heart to rejoice at the retributive justice of Heaven."

Great God—did an American utter such sentiments? There are two names which have been handed down to us, branded with infamy. Let the name of W. O. Duvall, the darkest traitor of all, with those of Benedict Arnold and Aaron Burr, go down to future ages, to be named only with a curse upon his memory.

Rev. T. Andrew Foss, of N. H., in an address before the American Anti-Slavery Society, at its meeting in N. York, May 13th, 1857, said:

"If the Angel Gabriel had done what their fathers did, he would have been a scoundrel for it. Their fathers placed within the Constitution, a provision for the rendition of Fugitive Slaves, and therein did a wicked thing. It would have been no more wrong for George the Third to put chains on George Washington, than it was for George Washington to put chains on the limbs of his Slaves. Their fathers had undoubtedly believed that they had made a government which would work beautifully; and that in a few years, Slavery would be extinct. But in that, they were deceived. The government was running as it was made to run, and it could not be made to run otherwise—so the Republicans might not boast what they would do, if they had the Government as it was, in the days of Washington and Jefferson. It was said in the good book, that the Lord sitteth on a high throne, and that all mankind are as grasshoppers before him. He expected that that included the President and Congress, and the Supreme Court and the Church. [Laughter.] Where Slavery and Freedom are put in one nation, there must be a fight; there must be an explosion, just as if fire and powder were brought together. There never was an hour when this blasphemous and infamous government should be made; and now, the hour was to be prayed for, when that disgrace to humanity should be dashed to pieces forever."

Here, we have another instance of that kind and Christian spirit (?) which seems to characterize the Abolition Clergy. Here, we see a man whose life *should be* as pure as the young morning air; not content with uttering sentiments of treason and discord, but putting forth the foulest blasphemy, reviling the written word of God, and false to every solemn vow that he has ever taken. "Oh, shame, where is thy blush!"

William Lloyd Garrison, a man who is honored and revered by the North; a man who never told the truth in his life; whose whole life has been a series of deceit and dishonor, private and public, thus addressed a meeting in New York city, on the first day of August, 1855. We wish our readers to examine this and reflect on it, for this speech was heartily approved and loudly cheered. He said:

"The issue is this: God Almighty has made it impossible from the beginning, for Liberty and Slavery to mingle together, or a Union to be founded between Abolitionists and Slave-Holders—between those who oppress and those who are oppressed. The Union is a lie; the American Union is a sham—an imposture—a covenant with death—an agreement with hell, and it is our business to call for a dissolution. Let that Union be accursed, wherein three millions and a-half of Slaves can be driven to unrequited toil by their masters.

"I will continue to experiment no longer—it is all madness. Let the Slave-Holding Union go, and Slavery will go with the Union down into the dust. If the Church is against disunion, and not on the side of the Slave, then I pronounce it as of the devil.

"I say, let us cease striking hands with thieves and adulterers, and give to the winds the rallying cry, 'No Union with Slave-Holders, socially or religiously, and up with the flag of disunion."

Again, he says:

"Justice and liberty, God and man demand the dissolution of this Slave-Holding Union, and the formation of a Northern Confederacy, in which Slave-Holders shall stand before the law as felons, and be treated as pirates. God and humanity demand a ballot-box in which the Slave-Holder shall never cast a ballot. In this, what State so prepared to lead as the old Bay State? She has already made it a penal offence to help to execute a law of the Union. I want to see the officers of the State brought into collision with those of the Union.

"No union with Slave-Holders. Up with the flag of disunion, that we may have a free and glorious Union of our own."

In an editorial in his paper, he says:

"Mark! How stands Massachusetts at this hour, in reference to the Union? Just where she ought to be—in an attitude of open hostility."

In the Liberator of June 20, 1856, he says:

"The United States Constitution is a covenant with death, an agreement with hell."

We have no comments to offer upon these effusions of William Lloyd Garrison. They need none. They are plain enough. We ask our readers to read them carefully, and to ponder over them.

We have no desire to dwell upon this arch-traitor and his treason, so we will pass on. The speeches and acts of Joshua R. Giddings, of Ohio, are as familiar as household words. If it were not that we wished to give him a place in our catalogue of traitors, we would not "touch him with a forty-foot pole."

In a speech delivered in the House of Representatives, on the 16th of March, 1854, he said:

"Sir, I would intimidate no one, but I tell you there is a spirit in the North that will set at defiance all the low and unworthy machinations of this Executive, and of the minions of its power. When the contest shall come; when the thunder shall roll and the lightning flash; when, in imitation of the Cuban bondmen, the Southern Slaves of the South shall feel that they are men; when they feel the stirring emotions of immortality, and recognize the stirring truths that they are men, and entitled to the rights which God has bestowed upon them; when the Slaves shall feel that, and when masters shall turn pale and tremble; when their dwellings shall smoke, and dismay sit on each countenance; then, Sir, I do not say 'we will laugh at your calamity, and mock when your fear cometh;' but I do say, when that time shall come, the lovers of our race will stand forth and exert the legitimate powers of this government for freedom. We shall then have Constitutional power to act for the good of our country, and do justice to the Slave.

"Then will we strike off the shackles from the limbs of the Slaves. That will be a period when this Government will have power to act between Slavery and freedom, and when it can make peace by giving freedom to the Slaves. And let me tell you, Mr. Speaker, that that time hastens. It is rolling forward. The President is exerting a power that will hasten it, though not intended by him. I hail it as I do the approaching dawn of that political and moral millenium, which, I am well assured, will come upon the world."

Mr. Giddings can offer no claim to originality, in announcing the doctrine, that in case a servile insurrection should occur, the Constitution would give the Federal Government power over the subject of Slavery! That then, the Federal Government would have power to crush this insurrection by the entire abolition of Slavery. We say that Mr. Giddings is not the author of this doctrine. He is merely a disciple. By reference to the "Annals of Congress," it will be seen that on the 2d day of January, 1841, John Quincy Adams, in the celebrated debate which took place that day, enunciated in plain and distinct terms, this abominable and unconstitutional doctrine. On the 9th of June, 1841, Mr. Adams repeated this doctrine.

Let us see what the Constitution says on this subject:

Section IV, of Article IV, plainly states: "1. The United States shall guarantee to every State in this Union, a Republican form of Government, and shall protect each of them against invasion! And, on application of the Legislature, or of the Executive, (when the Legislature cannot be convened,) *against domestic* violence."

Now it is well known that the Constitution was adopted in a spirit of compromise.

In 1842, in the case of Sprigg *vs.* the State of Pennsylvania, Mr. Justice McLean said:

"That the Constitution was adopted in a spirit of compromise, is a matter of history."

It is also known, that no article of the Constitution can legally be so construed as to render of no effect any other article of the Constitution.

The Constitution gives protection to Slavery and to Slave-Holders. The plea that the framers of the Constitution intended that it should be so construed as to let Slavery die out by degrees, is absurd. The very words show that such was not the design of our fathers—they show that our fathers expected that as long as the Constitution should last, Slavery would exist in its full vigor; and that they desired its protection by the Federal Government.

Now, let us see how the doctrine of Messrs. Adams and Giddings will work.

Let us suppose that an insurrection amongst the Slaves of the State of Virginia should occur. Let us suppose that the State is not able to suppress it. The Legislature is convened—the Federal Government is petitioned for aid. The Federal troops are sent to Virginia, and the insurrection is quelled. This is nothing more than the Constitution demands. The Federal Government has no right to refuse such aid. But can the mere fact of a rebellion against a sovereign State, quelled by the Federal Government, give to that power the right to alter or abolish any law of the State? Does an unsuccessful rebellion, do away with the laws already established, and make it necessary to enact others favorable to the purposes for which the rebellion was instituted?

But suppose that the insurrection is not quelled by the first aid rendered by the Federal Government. Does not the Constitution solemnly pledge the whole force of the Union to the suppression of "*domestic violence?*" Has the United States any right to enact laws for any of the sovereign States, without the consent of the people of such States? In case of such an insurrection, when the civil law could no longer prevail, it would be the duty of the Commander-in-Chief of the Federal Army to proclaim martial law, and when tranquillity should be again restored, the civil law would retake its place in all its former majesty and power. We contend that the Federal Government has no right to interfere in the domestic arrangements of the States. The Constitution, in requiring the Federal Government to protect the States, on their application, against all dangers, foreign and domestic, does nothing more than to require it to enforce and compel obedience to the laws of the States.

We contend, that neither Congress nor the State Legislatures have power to deprive the citizens of the Slave-Holding States of their property, without their consent.

But we have dwelt too long upon this, and we must hasten on. Wendell Phillips, in reviewing Mr. Webster's speech "on the Constitutional rights of the States," says:

"We are disunionists, not from any love of separate Confederacies, or as ignorant of the thousand evils that spring from neighboring and quarrelsome States, but we would get rid of this Union."

At an Abolition meeting, held in Boston, in May, 1849, this same Wendell Phillips makes the following startling declaration—men of the South, listen to it—be warned by it.

He says:

"We confess that we intend to trample under foot the Constitution of this country. Daniel Webster says: 'You are a law-abiding people;' that the glory of New England is, 'that it is a law-abiding community.' Shame on it, if this be true; even if the religion of New England sinks as low as its statute-book. *But I say, we are not a law-abiding community. God be thanked for it.*"

Hon. W. R. Sapp, of Ohio, in the House of Representatives, during the first session of the Thirty-fourth Congress, said:

"Yes, with that freedom, Fremont and Dayton emblazoned on the ample folds of our national banner, we will drive the base minions of Slavery from their control of the Government, and we will use its powers to build up our new government free from the taints of Slavery, and make America worthy of being the North Star of freedom, by which the eye of the exile can be guided with safety to the asylum of liberty."

This *Sapp-headed* gentleman has, in a few words, given us a very good history of the intentions of the Abolition party, and we give him quite a prominent place upon our list of traitors.

Gen. James Watson Webb, of the N. Y. Courier and Enquirer, an Abolition organ, "and we believe, the special organ of Senator Seward," says:

"If we, (the Republicans,) fail there, (at the ballot-box,) what then? We will drive it, (Slavery,) back, sword in hand; and, so help me God, believing that to be right, I am with them."

In a speech delivered in Cleveland, Ohio, in 1848, Mr. Seward declared:

"What then, you say nothing can be done for freedom because the public conscience is inert? Yes; much can be done, everything can be done."

In the same speech, he said:

"Correct your own error, that Slavery has any Constitutional guarantee which may not be released, and ought not to be relinquished."

In the same speech, he said:

"It (Slavery) can be, and it must be abolished, and you and I can and must do it."

In endorsing "The Impending Crisis," by Hinton Rowan Helper, (to (which we shall have occasion to refer hereafter,) Mr. Seward said:

"I have read the Impending Crisis of the South with great attention. It seems to me a work of great merit, rich, yet accurate in statistical information, and logical in analysis."

The Speaker of the New York House of Delegates, in referring to the Dred Scott case, said:

"I recognize no power under Heaven that can make a man a Slave. I recognize no law—no Constitution that can deprive a man of his personal rights and liberty; and I, a citizen of New York, am ready to place this State in that attitude.

"Suppose New York takes that ground; what then? Some talk of revolution, as if that were to be the dreaded result. Sir, I love the word. When this great State, with her three millions and upwards of freemen, takes that position, then I know that a death-blow is struck at African Slavery.

"I would not permit a fugitive from the South to be taken from our limits. What then? Will James Buchanan march troops into New York to coerce us into submission? We know that no attempt will be made thus to coerce this State when it takes this position."

We could continue to give such extracts, but we will not do so. We have no desire to pain our readers with the repetition of such treasonable sentiments. We confess that we are sick of it. We have only given them to show the position and sentiment of the North. What is the result of our labor? We find the North arrayed in a position hostile to the Union—and breathing the bitterest hatred against the South, and by their mad and unlawful course, endangering the peace, happiness and prosperity of the American Union. But it may be argued, that these extracts are only the sentiments of individuals. But we ask, do not these individuals represent the masses? Have not their sentiments been echoed and re-echoed, until the whole country resounds with them? Now that we have sustained our charge against the North—that it has been the cause of all of our internal discord and troubles—that from that quarter alone, has all of the treason against the Government proceeded. Now that we have proved their guilt, and rescued the South from the charges against it, let us look at some of the results of their teachings.

The first that we shall notice, is the *Kansas War*. The history of this war is so well known that we will not pause to make any comments upon it, or to enter into any description of it.

Now for the second: In May, 1858, a band of Abolition conspirators, under the lead of one John Brown, of Kansas notoriety, met in Chatham, Canada West, and entered into a conspiracy to overthrow the Federal Government of the United States, and to abolish Slavery. In order to give more dignity and force to their operations, they laid the foundation of, and adopted a Constitution for a Provisional Government, and elected all the officers required by the said Constitution. John Brown was chosen commander-in-chief of the armies of the said government. After transacting other business, the Convention adjourned. Brown moved to the State of Maryland, and settled in Washington County, on the border of the State. Here he collected arms and ammunition, which were furnished by Northern friends, and some of which, he purchased in the North, under false pretences. Here also, he received money from his friends at the North, and when all of his plans were completed, he, with twenty-one or two others, made their way stealthily into the little village of Harper's Ferry, on the border of Virginia, on the night of the 16th of October, 1859, and took possession of it, and of an important United States' Armory, containing about fifty thousand stands of different kinds of arms. After seizing the town and armory, which were entirely in a defenceless state—*guarded by only two unarmed men;* men were despatched to different places in the country, to seize the persons of several prominent gentlemen, and collect the Slaves. At daylight, on Monday, 17th, they were discovered, and the alarm given. The news spread with the speed of lightning. It reached Charlestown, ten miles distant, in an almost incredibly short time. The volunteers were promptly ordered under arms, and marched immediately to the scene of danger. The news being widely spread with intense rapidity, volunteers from all parts of the country hastened to the "seat of war." By noon, on Monday, the town of Harper's Ferry was completely invested. Between 3 and 4 o'clock, P. M., although in the midst of a severe storm, the conspirators were attacked—a portion of their number killed, and the rest driven into an engine-house in the armory yard. Here the United States claimed the right of dealing with them, and on Tuesday morning, the 18th, Col. R. E. Lee, of the U. S. Army, ordered a detachment of marines, under the immediate command of Lieut. Green, to storm the engine-house, and to take it. They did so, and all of the insurgents were either killed or taken prisoners. The prisoners were surrendered to the State of Virginia. Not one escaped but two who had been ordered away from the town by Brown on the first night of the seizure. They were afterwards captured. All the prisoners were given the benefit of a fair and impartial trial, convicted of treason, murder, and the attempt to excite insurrection, and have paid the penalty of their crimes on the gallows. It is, indeed, gratifying to us to be able to state that, in this *foray, not one single Slave or white man joined Brown; and the few captured by him soon escaped.* In the action between the troops and conspirators, five men were killed, and ten wounded. Among the former, were several gentlemen of worth.

The "Joint Committee of the General Assembly of Virginia," in their report on this subject, say:

"But in the opinion of your Committee, this is but a single, and comparatively unimportant chapter in the history of this outrage. They would cheerfully have undertaken the task of investigating the subject, in all its relations and ramifications, if they had possessed the power to compel the attendance of witnesses, who reside beyond the limits of the Commonwealth; but having no such power they are constrained to leave that branch of the investigation in the hands of the Committee of the Senate of the United States. Your Committee have no hesitation, however, in expressing the opinion, from the evidence before them, that many others, besides the parties directly engaged in the raid at Harper's Ferry, are deeply implicated as aiders and abettors and accessories, before the fact, with full knowledge of the guilty purposes of their confederates. Some of these, like Gerrit Smith, of New York, Dr. S. G. Howe, of Boston, —— Sanborn, and Thaddeus Hyatt, of New York, and probably others, are represented to have held respectable positions in society; but whatever may have been their social standing heretofore they must henceforth, in the esteem of all good men, be branded as the guilty confederates of thieves, murderers and traitors.

"The evidence before your Committee is sufficient to show the existence, in a number of Northern States, of a wide-spread conspiracy, not merely against Virginia, but against the peace and security of all the Southern States. But the careful erasure of names and dates from many of the papers, found in Brown's possession, renders it difficult to procure legal evidence of the guilt of the parties implicated. The conviction of the existence of such a conspiracy, is deepened by the sympathy with the culprits, which has been manifested by large numbers of persons in the Northern States, and by the disposition which your Committee are satisfied did exist to rescue them from the custody of the law."

This report continues:

"This invasion of a sovereign State by citizens of other States, confederated with subjects of a foreign government, presents matters for grave consideration. It is an event without a parallel in the history of our country. And when we remember, that the incursion was marked by distinct geographical features; that it was made by citizens of Northern States on a Southern State; that all the countenance and encouragement which it received, and all the material aid which was extended to it, were by citizens of Northern States; and that its avowed object was to make war upon and overthrow an institution, intimately interwoven with all the interests of the Southern States, and constituting an essential element of their social and political systems—an institution which has existed in Virginia for more than two centuries, and which is recognized and guaranteed by the mutual covenants between the North and the South, embodied in the Constitution of the United States, every thoughtful mind must be filled with deep concern and anxiety for the future peace and security of the country."

Such are the facts connected with

John Brown's foray into Virginia, which we have styled the result of the Abolition teachings of the North.

Indeed, Senator Wilson, of Massachusetts, said at Syracuse, New York, Nov. 28th, 1859, "The Harper's Ferry Outbreak was the consequence of the teachings of Republicanism."

They have burst upon the country like a thunderbolt; they have, at last, roused the South to a true sense of her danger and she is preparing to meet it

But it may be argued, that the evi dence before "the Joint Committee of the General Assembly of Virginia," was not sufficient to cause them to report, that a strong feeling of hostility towards, and a widely-spread conspiracy against, the South now exists in the North. This argument is false. But just for curiosity, let us see what the Northern press and pulpit say in regard to this matter:

The New York Evening Post, an Abolition sheet, in its issue of December 3d, 1859, thus speaks of the execution of John Brown on the previous day:

"THE EXECUTION AND ITS EFFECTS.—The manner in which popular feeling has manifested itself at the North, with regard to Brown's execution, proves the wisdom of his own remark, when he said, he could, in no way, so well serve the cause he had at heart, as by hanging for it. We do not so much allude to the outward manifestations of respect for his name and memory, the devotion of the hour of his death to prayer in a great number of churches, the tolling of bells in many towns, the firing of minute guns in others—though these have in themselves a marked significance—as to the pity which every one, whose pity is worth having, has openly expressed for the old man's fate; the sympathy which almost every one seemed glad to avow for his simple and manly virtues, and the silence with which, for the sake of those virtues, the faults and follies of a wild and wayward life have been covered almost by the whole community.

"The death of a criminal on the gallows, of whom half the nation speaks tenderly, and whose last hours the prayers and fastings of many thousands of sincere religious men have sought to hallow, is certainly not an incident to be dismissed with newspaper paragraphs.

"He has been dismissed from the bar with his judgment indeed impeached, but with no weightier condemnation of his acts, than that they were marked by folly. In war all is folly which does not succeed; the rule is harsh perhaps, but necessary. Napoleon said, Leonidas was no doubt a very fine fellow, 'but he let himself be turned at Thermôpylæ.' Virginia, to be sure, thinks Brown more a knave than fool; but in this matter the Virginians bear much the same relation to him, in the eyes of the world at large, that Francis Joseph bears to Kossuth. A large part of the civilized public will, as a large part of the world does already, lay on his tomb the honors of martyrdom; and while those honors remain there, his memory will be more terrible to Slave-Holders than his living presence could have been; because it will bring recruits to his cause, who never would have served under his banner while he was wielding carnal weapons.

"If all these be facts, they are, no doubt, unpleasant facts for every one who has the future welfare of his country at heart, to contemplate. But that is certainly not a reason for trying to hide.

"It is, therefore, we think, a sign, not of national decline, but of growth in all the real elements of national greatness, that sorrowing hundreds of thousands should have been found to overlook this man's errors, in admiration for his heroism, for his fortitude, and of his hatred of oppression. It is to such qualities as these, and not a holy horror of mere disorder, that we owe our existence as a nation; and when the day comes in which no man will be found in

America to cry bravo when he sees them, our final extinction will not be very far distant."

The following extracts are from a discourse preached in the Unitarian Church, Dover, N. H., to a large and approving congregation:

"No, it is not true, that the conflict of Harper's Ferry is the beginning of a civil war. That would be like saying the capture of Yorktown was the beginning of the Revolutionary struggle. The meaning of that new sign, is this: Freedom for ten years weakly standing on the defensive, and for ten years defeated, has now become the assailant, and has now gained the victory. The Bunker Hill of our second Revolution has been fought, and the second Warren has paid the glorious forfeit of his life."

" * * * * If an honest expression of the wishes of the North could be taken to-morrow, John Brown would be the people's candidate for the next Presidency, and he would receive a million of votes.

" * * * * * * Editors and politicians call Brown mad, and so he is to them; for he has builded his manly life of more than three-score years upon the faith and fear of God—a thing which editors and politicians, from the time of Christ till now, have always regarded as a full proof of insanity. One such man makes total depravity impossible, and proves that American greatness died not with Washington. The gallows from which he ascends to Heaven, will be in our politics what the cross is in our religion—the sign and symbol of supreme self-devotedness; and from his sacrificial blood, the temporary salvation of four millions of people shall yet spring. On the second day of December, he is to be strangled in a Southern prison, for obeying the Sermon on the Mount. But to be hanged in Virginia, is like being crucified in Jerusalem—it is the last tribute which sin pays to virtue."

We have no desire to give more of these extracts. The above are the *mildest* that we have been able to discover.

We think that we have sustained our position, and we leave this part of our subject to notice that most infamous production known as the "Impending Crisis of the South, by Hinton Rowan Helper, of North Carolina." It would be difficult for us to describe the feelings with which we have perused this abominable and shameful production; it is more like the work of a fiend than of a human being. Professedly a Southerner at heart, Helper is a villain—of the darkest dye. He was driven out of North Carolina on account of his dishonest and villainous propensities.

Some years ago, he published a Pro-Slavery work, entitled "the Land of Gold," but not finding it profitable, he went over to the more lucrative side.

We will not dwell upon it any longer than to give a brief summary of the doctrines contained in it. These are as follows:

"Slave-Holders are a nuisance."

"It is our imperative duty to abate nuisances."

"We propose to exterminate this catalogue from beginning to end."

"We believe that thieves are, as a general thing, less amenable to the moral law than Slave-Holders."

"Slave-Holders are more criminal than common murderers."

"Slave-Holders and Slave-Traders are, as a general thing, unfit to occupy any honorable station in life."

"That they deserve to be at once reduced to a parallel with the basest criminals that lie fettered within the cells of our public prisons."

"Were it possible that the whole number (of Slave-Holders) could be gathered together, and transferred into four equal bands of licensed robbers, ruffians, thieves, and murderers, society, we feel assured, would suffer less from their atrocities then, than it does now."

On page 76 of the Compendium, he gives "the principles which," as he conceives, "should govern them in their *patriotic warfare*."

"*First.*—Thorough Organization and Independent Political Action on the part of the Non-Slave-Holding Whites of the South.

"*Second.*—Ineligibility of Pro-Slavery-Holders. Never another vote for any one who advocates the Retention and Perpetuation of Human Slavery.

"*Third.*—No Co-operation with Pro-Slavery Politicians. No Fellowship with them in Religion. No Affiliation with them in Society.

"*Fourth.*—No Patronage to Pro-Slavery Merchants. No Guestship in Slave-waiting Hotels. No Fees to Pro-Slavery Lawyers. No Employment of Pro-Slavery Physicians. No Audience to Pro-Slavery Parsons.

"*Fifth.*—No more Hiring of Slaves by Non-Slave-Holders.

"*Sixth.*—Abrupt Discontinuance of Subscription to Pro-Slavery Newspapers.

"*Seventh.*—The Greatest Possible Encouragement to Free White Labor."

This book has been endorsed by numerous members of Congress, and leading men of the Abolition party. It has been heartily approved and earnestly recommended by them. We have no desire to enter upon a review of the book. We feel too much contempt for the book and its author, to wish to notice it further. It has been ably reviewed, and its arguments triumphantly refuted. We think that we have made a very bad case against the North; and, in doing so, we have simply stated "plain and unvarnished facts."

But it may be offered, as a last argument, that although the Northern people are so unfriendly to the Union and to us, that the States themselves are not. Let us see: The Committee on the Harper's Ferry Outrages, in their Report to the Legislature of Virginia, furnish us with ample information here. They say:

"If we turn to the legislative action of the Northern States, in which that (the Abolition) party has obtained the ascendancy, we find that it is in strict conformity with their mischievous dogmas. Their statute-books are filled with enactments, conceived in a spirit of hostility to the institutions of the South, at war with the true intent and meaning of the Federal Compact, and adopted for the express purpose of rendering nugatory some of the express covenants of the Constitution of the United States."

The report then goes on to give a brief sketch of some of the most prominent features of the Anti-Slavery Laws.

MAINE.

"By the laws of this State it is provided, that if a Fugitive Slave shall be arrested, he shall be defended by the Attorney for the Commonwealth, and all expenses of such defence paid out of the public treasury. The use of all State and County jails, and of all buildings belonging to the State, are forbidden for the reception or securing of Fugitive Slaves, and all officers are forbidden, under heavy penalties, from arresting or aiding in the arrest, of such fugitives. If a Slave-Holder, or any person, shall unlawfully seize or confine a Fugitive Slave, he shall be liable to be imprisoned for not more than five years, or fined not exceeding $1,000. If a Slave-Holder takes a Slave into the State, the Slave is thereby made free; and if the master undertake to exercise any control over him, he is subjected to imprisonment for not less than one year, or fined not exceeding $1,000.

"The Dred Scott decision of the Supreme Court has been declared unconstitutional, and many offensive and inflammatory resolutions have been passed by the Legislature.

NEW HAMPSHIRE.

"Your Committee have not had access to a complete series of the laws of this State, but a general index which has been consulted, shows that a law exists, by which all Slaves entering the State, either with or without the consent of their masters, are declared free; and any attempt to capture or hold them is declared to be a felony.

VERMONT.

"This State seems to have entirely forgotten the conservative and law-abiding sentiment which governed its action in the earliest period of her history."

"Her law now forbids all citizens, or officers of the State, from executing or assisting to execute, the Fugitive Slave Law, or to arrest a Fugitive Slave, under penalty of imprisonment for not less than one year, or a fine not exceeding $1,000. It also forbids the use of all public jails or buildings for the purpose of securing such Slaves. The Attorneys for the State are directed, at public expense, to defend and procure to be discharged every person arrested as a Fugitive Slave. The *habeas corpus* act also provides that Fugitive Slaves shall be tried by jury, and interposes other obstacles to the execution of the Fugitive Slave Law.

"The law further provides, that all persons capturing or seizing or confining any person as a Fugitive Slave, shall be confined in the State prison not more than ten years, and fined not exceeding $1,000. Every person held as a Slave, who shall be brought into the State, is declared free; and all persons who shall hold or attempt to hold, as a Slave, any persons so brought into the State, in any form, or for any time, however short, shall be confined in the State prison not less than one nor more than fifteen years, and fined not exceeding $2,000. The Legislature has also passed sundry offensive resolutions.

MASSACHUSETTS.

"The laws of this State forbid, under heavy penalties, her citizens, and State and County officers, from executing the Fugitive Slave Law, or from arresting a Fugitive Slave, or from aiding in either; and denies the use of her jails and public buildings for such purposes.

"The Governor is required to appoint Commissioners in every County, to aid Fugitive Slaves in recovering their freedom, when proceeded against as Fugitive Slaves, and all costs attending such proceedings are ordered to be paid by the State.

"Any person who shall remove, or attempt to remove, or come into the State with the intention to remove, or assist in removing, any person who is not a Fugitive Slave, within the meaning of the Constitution, is liable to punishment by fine of not less than $1,000 nor more than $5,000, and imprisoned not less than one nor more than five years.

"The *habeas corpus* act gives trial by jury to Fugitive Slaves, and interposes other unlawful impediments to the execution of the Fugitive Slave Law. Her Legislature has also passed violent and offensive resolutions.

CONNECTICUT.

"This State, which, as late as 1840, tolerated Slavery within her own borders, as appears by the census of that year, prohibits, under severe penalties, all her officers from executing the Fugitive Slave Law, and vacates all official acts which may be done by them in attempting to execute that law.

"By the Act of 1854, Section 1, it is provided, that every person who shall falsely and maliciously declare, represent, or pretend that any person entitled to freedom is a Slave, or owes service or labor to any person or persons, with the intent to procure, or aid or assist in procuring, the forcible removal of such free person from this State, as a Slave, shall pay a fine of $5,000, and shall be imprisoned for five years in the State prison.

"'Section 2. In all cases arising under this act, the truth of any declaration, representation, or pretence, that any person being or having been in this State, is or was a Slave, owes or did owe service or labor to any other person or persons, shall not be deemed proved, except by the testimony of at least two credible witnesses, testifying to facts directly tending to the truth of such declaration, pretence or representation, or by legal evidence equivalent thereto.'

"Section 3—subjects to a fine of $5,000, and imprisoned in the State prison for five years, all who shall seize any person entitled to freedom, with the intent to have such person held in Slavery.

"Section 4—prohibits the admission of depositions in all cases under this act, and provides, that if any witness testifies falsely *in behalf of the party accused*, and prosecuted under this act, he shall be fined $5,000, and imprisoned five years in the State prison. This law is, in the opinion of your Committee, but little short of an invitation to perjury, by imposing no penalties on false swearing *against* the accused.

"The resolutions of the Legislature are disorganizing and offensive.

RHODE ISLAND.

"The statutes of Rhode Island provide, that any one who transports, or causes to be transported, by land or water, any person lawfully inhabiting therein, to any place without the limits of the State, except by due course of law, shall be imprisoned not less than one nor more than ten years. They also prohibit all officers from aiding in executing the Fugitive Slave Law, or arresting a Fugitive Slave; and deny the use of her jails and public buildings for securing any such fugitives.

NEW YORK.

"This State has enacted, that any person who shall, without lawful authority, remove or attempt to remove from this State any Fugitive Slave, shall forfeit to the party aggrieved five hundred dollars, and be imprisoned not exceeding ten years in the State prison; and all accessories after the fact are also liable to imprisonment.

"The *habeas corpus* act provides that Fugitive Slaves shall be entitled to trial by jury, and makes it the duty of all the Commonwealth's Attorneys to defend Fugitive Slaves at the expense of the State.

"New York has a fugitive law of her own, which is of no practical use, and has forbidden her judicial officers from proceeding under any other law.

"Prior to 1841, persons not inhabitants of the State, were allowed to take their Slaves with them, and keep them in the State for a limited time, but the law has been repealed.

NEW JERSEY.

"Her law provides that, if any person shall forcibly take away from this State, any man, woman, or child, bond or free, into another State, he shall be punished by a fine not exceeding $1,000, or by imprisonment at hard labor not exceeding five years, or both.

"The *habeas corpus* act gives a trial by jury to Fugitive Slaves, and all judicial officers are prohibited from acting under any other than the law of New Jersey.

PENNSYLVANIA.

"Prior to 1847, non-resident owners of Slaves were allowed to retain them in Pennsylvania, not exceeding six months. In 1847, this privilege was revoked. Slaves are also allowed to testify in all cases in the Courts of Pennsylvania. It is further provided by law, that any person 'who violently or tumultuously seizes upon any negro or mulatto, and carries such negro away to any place, either with or without the intention of taking such negro before a District or Circuit Judge, shall be fined not exceeding $1,000, and imprisoned in the County jail not exceeding three months.' The law also punishes, with a heavy fine and imprisonment in the penitentiary, any person who may forcibly carry away, or attempt to carry away, any free negro or mulatto from the State. The sale of Fugitive Slaves is prohibited under heavy penalties, and a trial by jury is secured to Fugitive Slaves, in violation of the laws of the United States.

ILLINOIS.

"Illinois has prohibited, under pain of imprisonment of not less than one nor more than seven years, any person from stealing or arresting any Slave, with the design of taking such Slave out of the State, without first having established his claim thereto, according to the laws of the United States. These penalties will he incurred by the master who pursues his Slave across the border, and apprehends him without waiting for the action of the Commissioner or Court.

INDIANA.

"Some of the laws of this State are favorable to the recovery of fugitives from labor. But the law as to kidnapping is similar to that of Illinois, as above noted, except that the penalties are greater. The fine is not less than $100 nor more than $5,000, and the term of imprisonment not less than two nor more than fourteen years.

OHIO.

"In 1858, the most offensive parts of the laws of this State were repealed. It is understood, however, that measures are in contemplation, if they have not already been initiated, to re-enact them.

MICHIGAN.

"The laws of this State are peculiarly obnoxious to criticism. They not only deny the use of jails and public buildings to secure Fugitive Slaves, and require the Attorneys for the Commonwealth to defend them, at the expense of the State, but the law of Connecticut, in relation to the punishment of persons falsely alleging others to be Slaves, is adopted with the addition, that any person who carries a Slave into this State, claiming him as such, shall be punished by imprisonment in the State prison for a period not exceeding ten years, or by a fine not exceeding $1,000.

"The *habeas corpus* act provides for trial by jury, of claims to Fugitive Slaves.

"Resolutions have also been adopted by the Legislature urging the repeal of the Fugitive Slave Law, and the prohibition of Slavery in the District of Columbia and the Territories.

WISCONSIN.

"Following the example of her sister States of the North, in parts of their hostile legislation, this State has, in some particulars, gone beyond all the rest. She has directed her District Attorneys, in all cases of Fugitive Slaves, to appear for and defend them, at the expense of the State. She has required the issue of the writ of *habeas corpus*, on the mere statement of the District Attorney, that a person in custody is detained as a Fugitive Slave, and requires all her judicial and executive officers, who have reason to believe that a person is about to be arrested on such ground, to give notice to the District Attorney of the County where the person resides. If a Judge in vacation fails to discharge the arrested Fugitive Slave on *habeas corpus*, an appeal is allowed to the next Circuit Court.

"Trial by jury is to be granted at the election of either party, and all costs of trial, which would otherwise fall on the fugitive, are assumed by the State.

"A law has also been enacted, similar to that of Connecticut, for the punishment of one who shall falsely and maliciously declare any person to be a Fugitive Slave, with intent to aid in procuring the forcible removal of such person from the State as a Slave. A section is added to the provisions of this Connecticut law, for the punishment by imprisonment in the State prison, of any person who shall obstruct the execution of a warrant issued under it, or aid in the escape of the person accused. Another section forbids the enforcement of a judgment recovered for the violation of 'the Fugitive Slave Act,' by the sale of any real or personal property in the State, and makes its provisions applicable to judgments theretofore rendered.

"The law relative to kidnapping punishes the forcible seizure, without lawful authority, of any person of color, with intent to cause him to be sent out of the State, or sold as a Slave, or in any manner to transfer his service or labor, or the actual selling or transferring the service of such person, by imprisonment in the State prison from one to two years, or by fine from $500 to $1,000. The consent of the person seized, sold, or transferred, not to be a defence, unless it appear to the jury that it was not obtained by fraud, nor extorted by duress or by threats.

IOWA.

"The law of this State is similar to that of Indiana, except that here there seems to be no direct provision favoring the recovery of Fugitive Slaves. Like that of Indiana and Illinois, the law as to kidnapping may be so construed, as greatly to obstruct the arrest of such fugitive. The maximum of punishment is, however, something less, being five years in the State prison, and a fine of $1,000.

"Offensive resolutions have also been adopted by its Legislature.

MINNESOTA.

"What is to be objected to the legislation of this State is, that there is no sufficient recognition of the right of the master to recover his Fugitive Slave; and, consequently, even if such was not the *design* of the omission, the way is left open for the perversion of the law relative to the writ of *habeas corpus*, to the injury of Slave owners."

Such, then, is a brief summary of the hostile laws of the Non-Slave-Holding States, and we offer them as our answer to the last argument submitted to us.

We have, in a larger space than we originally intended, given a brief history of the rise, the progress, and the acts of the Abolition Party. We have seen that their whole course has been one calculated to bring about a rupture of all good feelings between the two great sections of the country; to produce disunion and discord; and to excite a just alarm on the part of the Slave-Holding States.

We have seen them sustained in this course by legislative enactments and resolutions.

The picture of the North that we have drawn is a dark one, but it is not exaggerated—it is terrible, but true! We have drawn it in strong colors—but we have done so in no spirit of hatred to the North, or a desire to produce a sectional hatred against it in the South. We have done so, only to show the true position of the North—to rescue the South from the charges of treason, disunion, and sectional strife; and, finally, to point out to her her danger, and to warn her to prepare to meet it.

We have endeavored to show the aggressions of the North upon Southern Rights. During the long period in which the Slavery question has been agitated, the South has never presented itself in any attitude but that of peace; it has demanded of the North no sacrifice of Territory, or of its Constitutional rights; it has uttered no cries of treason, or threats of disunion; it has pointed to the Union, and implored peace, "when there was no peace;" it has met every aggression upon its rights with compromises and sacrifices; it has submitted to insult and injury, because it hoped for a returning sense of justice at the North; it has said to the North—"Do not menace our beloved Union—remember whose work it was;" it has said to the North—"Go on, increase and prosper. Make your country as proud and as glorious as you will; we will rejoice in your happiness, for you are a part of us." It has asked—nay, it has implored—to be left alone in the enjoyment of its Constitutional rights and privileges.—To be let alone! Often and earnestly has this prayer gone forth;—and what was the result? Fresh aggressions—new attacks upon its rights.

Now, the South has sacrificed—has compromised every thing but its homes and its honor. It has awakened to a true sense of its danger and its rights. It has ceased to be a suppliant, and it now *demands* to be left alone in the enjoyment of its rights and blessings.—To be let alone! It has determined to enforce these rights, if it must be, with the sword.

Long suffering, long oppressed—for a long time patiently waiting for a restoration of peace and harmony—but disappointed in her expectations—the South has seen that the only course left for her to pursue is, Resistance to Anti-Slavery Aggression.

It is well known that the only protection to the South which now exists, is the Act of Congress passed September 12th, 1850, and known as "The Fugitive Slave Law,"—and this sole protection is made null and void by the unconstitutional laws of the Free States. These States array themselves in open hostility towards the South, and defy her to maintain her rights. And, even now, the North has demanded, with unblushing front, the repeal of this law, and the Legislature of Massachusetts, by an official act, have sanctioned this demand. What course should the South pursue in regard to this? is the question which will at once present itself to every mind. That there is danger now threatening the South no one will deny. It would be foolish—aye, worse than foolish, for us to shut our eyes and profess not to see it as it stares us in the face. It is a danger of no trifling character—a danger of such a character that it becomes necessary to meet it, and to meet it at once. Delay is dangerous; every moment that we lose in pausing to consider, our cause is being weakened, whilst that of our aggressors is being visibly strengthened. How then can this danger be met? By prompt and immediate action. Let the South organize her militia, and use every possible means to place herself in a state of defence.—But in all of her actions let her be united and not divided. Union will give her strength. Let her encourage and develop her domestic resources; let her take such steps as to lay the foundation of a commercial and manufacturing system, which shall be independent of the North; let her learn to rely upon herself—God has given us a rich and fertile land, a land which can be made to yield enough for our own support, and for the support of others. We have amongst us all the elements of greatness—political, commercial and domestic. We can make the South equal to any country in the world, and we must do it. When the South is organized and armed, let the *entire* South demand of their sister States at the North, what course they intend pursuing with regard to Slavery: let her demand a recognition by them of her rights, and a pledge for their security and protection; let her demand (and she has a right to do so) an immediate and unconditional repeal of all the unconstitutional and hostile laws upon the subject of Slavery that now exist in the Free States. Let her make these demands mildly, but firmly; let her not yield or compromise one single point, but let her insist upon the unconditional acknowledgment and protection of her rights. We say, let her do this, and it may be that by facing the danger she may avert it, and this Union be perpetuated. But if her demands be refused, (and God grant that they may not be,) she has but one alternative left, she must withdraw from the Union, peaceably if possible, violently if it must be so. Let the result be what it may, she can, in such a case, remain in the Union only by the sacrifice of her rights; of her greatness; of her honor; and, it may be, of her children.

She has proved her devotion to the Union sufficiently; she must now look to her own safety. When the Union cannot secure her her rights and privileges; when it is used as an instrument to attack, degrade and crush her, it will be already virtually annulled, and all that will be left to be done, will be for the South to withdraw from it, to form a government for herself, and to rely upon herself for protection.

We have no desire to see this Union destroyed, but as a last resort; and most earnestly do we pray, that the Divine Governor of the World will so order all things, as to secure to us, a perpetual Union of EQUAL INDEPENDENT SOVEREIGN STATES.

We have already shown how terrible and how dangerous to the Union is the existence of the Abolition Party. We have counselled resistance to them. Before we take leave of our readers we would most earnestly entreat them to resist, by every means in their power, the election of an Abolition President. We implore them, for the sake of the Union; for the sake of the South, to resist it. Resist it, because when an Abolition traitor fills the President's Chair, the last hope of the South will be gone. An Abolition President can wield a terrible power against the South. He can fill every office in his gift with his fellow-traitors; he can strengthen the hands of his party so effectually, as to prevent the South from ever being able to defeat it. He can begin to turn African Slaves into Freemen, by turning Southern Freemen into Slaves; and the South will then, in self-defence, be compelled to withdraw from the Union—but, alas! in what a shattered condition.

Men of the South, we appeal to you to be men indeed. Look to the interests of the South. Guard them with sleepless vigilance. May God give you strength so to act, as to secure the greatest possible good for your country and the Union.

The South has now an opportunity offered her, which, in our humble judgment, she ought not to neglect. The State of South Carolina proposes to her sister Southern States, that they shall each appoint delegates to a Convention, to be held in Atlanta, Georgia.

The object of this Convention is not to dissolve the Union, nor even to endanger its safety. It is a Convention, called for the purpose of bringing the entire South into a *united* body, and to devise some means for securing the greatest possible happiness and stability to the entire country, and to adopt measures for the enforcement of the rights of the South.

The following letter from the Governor of South Carolina, fully and ably sets forth the objects of the proposed Convention.

EXECUTIVE DEPARTMENT,
Unionville, S. C., Feb. 3, 1860.

TO HIS EXCELLENCY, THOMAS H. HICKS,
Governor of Maryland.

DEAR SIR:

Yours of the 26th of January, acknowledging the receipt of the resolutions unanimously adopted by the State of South Carolina, was received yesterday; and I must be permitted to correct a very grave error into which you have fallen in relation to them. You speak of the resolutions as "requesting this State (Maryland) to join in the appointment of Deputies to a Convention of the Slave-Holding States, for their united action in regard to secession from the Union." If there is anything in the resolutions proposing a "secession from the Union," I am unable find it, and deny that South Carolina proposes any such measures to Maryland, or her other co-States. By re-examining the resolutions, you will find that all that South Carolina proposes is, "that the Slave-Holding States should immediately meet together to concert measures for the united action," and that it is a forced and unwarrantable construction of the resolutions to say, that "concerted action" means secession from the Union. I belong to that class of politicians who have been denounced as "fire-eaters," and never, for a moment, have I desired a dissolution of the Union, if our rights in the Union are respected and our equality recognized. And I solemnly believe that the very best way to preserve the Union, is for the Southern States to meet and insist upon their rights, and to act in concert in defending them. If the South were united, they could preserve the Union, and at the same time have their rights respected and recognized. It is because the Southern States have acted with so much jealousy and distrust towards each other, that the North has been able to encroach upon their rights, and war upon their institutions. If I desired a dissolution of the Union, and wished to effect it, nothing would please me more than the refusal of the Slave-Holding States to meet in Convention: for then the North will continue its aggressions, and some of the Slave-Holding States, goaded to madness, will secede, preferring to be held as conquered provinces rather than become voluntary slaves. Speaking for myself, I would rather "South Carolina should become the cemetery of freemen than the habitation of Slaves," and animated by these sentiments, our people never will submit to inequality and degradation.

With great respect,
I am, yours, &c.,
WM. H. GIST.

This letter explains fully and ably the objects of the proposed Convention. A perpetuation of the Union, and to advise the South how to act in the present critical condition of the country.

The Minority of the Joint Committee of the Virginia Legislature, upon the South Carolina Resolutions, speak of this as follows:

"We submit with great deference that if '*concurrent action and efficient co-operation*' upon the part of the Southern States be desirable, *for the purpose of protecting the rights and liberties of the people and preserving the Federal Union*, they may be *most safely* and certainly obtained through the agency of an assemblage, which can exercise no legitimate power, except to 'debate and advise.' In the opinion of the Minority of your Committee, the want of power in the proposed Conference to do more than '*debate and advise*,' so far from constituting an objection to it, furnishes a strong argument in its favor, and gives assurance to the timid, that none of the evils, so hastily predicted by the opponents of the measure, can possibly result from the proposed Conference of the Southern States." * * * * * *

"It is not in the South alone that we

look for the happiest results from such a Conference. We believe that the conservative masses of the North will be aroused by such a Conference as we propose; that concurrent action, and efficient co-operation, may be anticipated from them, and that they will cordially unite with us to save that Union which they, in common with us, regard as the 'palladium of our political safety and prosperity.' We repeat then, that it is with no spirit or desire to weaken or destroy the bonds that bind together the States of the American Union, but to strengthen them, that we urge the General Assembly of Virginia to respond to the invitation of South Carolina, by sending delegates to the proposed Conference. Let Virginia send such men as she may safely confide in for prudence, patriotism and discretion; such men as will counsel wisely and firmly—who, whilst they make known the policy deemed by Virginia best suited to the emergency for the common defence, will urge upon our Southern Sisters, the adoption of that policy, and invoke them to remain with us in the Union; and exhaust every peaceful and constitutional means for its preservation and restoration, before they withdraw from it, and involve themselves and us in the disaster of its overthrow.

"We know full well that the effort has been made, and will be made again, for purposes best known to those who engage in it, to stigmatize as Disunionists all who think that the Southern States may and should meet together, and counsel for their common safety, and for redress of their common grievances. If any amongst us are weak enough to be frightened from their propriety by such false clamor, we have only to say for ourselves, that the application of such an epithet cannot deter us from urging a measure, upon the success of which we conscientiously and firmly believe the salvation of this Union essentially depends. It will not restrain us from seeking, by such peaceful and constitutional means, to obtain for Virginia her full, equal, and constitutional rights under the Federal Government.

"We also know it has been represented by some, that it is the avowed object of South Carolina to bring about this Conference for the purpose of dissolving the Union. Neither in her resolutions, nor in the address of her Commissioner, can any warrant for such an assertion be found. South Carolina has spoken in her resolutions, and through her Commissioner, with that candor and frankness becoming the occasion, and her chivalrous character. Let her speak for herself, and let an enlightened and candid people judge whether she has not been grossly misrepresented in her purposes and declarations.

"The preamble to her resolutions announces that, in 1852, by her ordinance, she 'affirmed her right to secede from the Confederacy whenever the occasion should arise justifying her, in her own judgment, in taking that step; and in the resolution adopted by her Convention, declared, that she forbore the immediate exercise of that right from considerations of expediency only.'

"Now, we demand to know whether, in the assertion of the right to secede from the Union, South Carolina has rendered herself obnoxious to the charge of seeking to dissolve the Union? If so, how stands Virginia? Does she not maintain now, has she not always maintained, the right to secede under such circumstances? South Carolina has then affirmed the right, but desisted from the act of secession. And why did she desist? Because Virginia, by her resolutions of December, 1851, '*earnestly and affectionately appeals to her sister State of South Carolina, to desist from any meditated secession on her part, which cannot but tend to the destruction of the Union, and the loss to all the States of the benefits that spring from it.*'

"The preamble further declares, that since that declaration was made, 'the assaults upon the institution of Slavery, and upon the rights and equality of the Southern States, have unceasingly continued, with increasing violence, and in new and more alarming forms.' Is this not true? What did South Carolina, by her resolutions, declare and propose? '*Still* deferring to her Southern sisters,' she 'respectfully announces' to them, that it is 'her deliberate judgment that the Slave-Holding States should immediately meet together, *to concert measures for united action.*' Secondly, she requested all the Southern States to appoint deputies; and, lastly, she sent a Special Commissioner to Virginia, 'to express to the authorities the cordial sympathy of the people of South Carolina with the people of Virginia, and their *earnest desire to unite with them in measures of common defence,*' and to urge upon her the appointment of Commissioners to 'a Conference of the Slave-Holding States.'

"It will be observed, that the Report of the Majority concedes the necessity of '*decisive measures,*' '*concurrent action,*' and '*efficient co-operation*' among the Southern States. The resolutions of South Carolina recognize the necessity for '*united action,*' and the adoption of 'measures of common defence,' by the Southern States. In other words, they desire substantially the same thing, but propose different modes of obtaining it. What the one proposes to accomplish by the separate action of the several State Legislatures, *without previous concert,* the other proposes to accomplish by *united action* upon the part of all, *ascertaining first, by means of a Conference,* what measures are proper to be concerted for the common defence of all.

"The only advantage claimed by the Majority for their plan, over the one proposed by the resolutions of South Carolina is, that by it the common object may be more *safely* obtained. We affirm then, without the fear of successful contradiction, that no warrant is to be found in the preamble and resolutions of South Carolina for the charge, that the Conference is a Disunion measure. Let us for a moment, then, examine the proposition as explained by her Commissioner. In his address, he says:

"'But why waste our time in surmise, when realities are thrust openly before us? Can any one mistake the roaring of the storm at Washington? Has the column of the Republican Party there shown any sign of wavering? Was ever such a spectacle presented to this country before? There are plainly exhibited the dire effects of this array of sections—and there, in that conflict for the mastery, is foreshadowed that real conflict between the States, to which we are soon to be summoned.

"'Will you undertake that conflict singly, or shall we act in concert? That is the great question which I am commissioned to ask. In 1847, and again in 1849, your judgment pronounced in favor of 'concerted action.' We have adopted your judgment—and we come now to propose the Conference. From the Federal Government, as it stands, we can expect nothing. From the Northern States we have been repelled with denunciations. Our only resource then, is in ourselves; and among ourselves union is strength.

"'The great and leading argument in favor of a Conference is, that it is the proper step in any contingency. It is a measure which will preserve the Union, if it can constitutionally be preserved; and if it cannot, it is the proper preparatory step for Southern defence. Those who desire the maintenance of the Union, must perceive, that nothing is more likely to drive back the aggressions of the North, and to restore to us our rights, than the exhibition of a united and determined purpose of resistance. And those who believe that the Union cannot be preserved, will easily perceive that a Southern Conference is a necessary step to effective Southern defence.

This measure ought, therefore, to unite all parties, excepting alone that (if there be any such) which favors unconditional submission.'

" Again he says:

"'On the other hand, those who believe in the efficacy of measures of restriction and commercial independence, must perceive that such measures would be far more effective if taken in concert. What benefit would result from non-importation into Richmond and Norfolk, if Edenton and Newbern and Beaufort received Northern goods as before? and what good effect would restrictions at Charleston serve, if Savannah should decline concurrence? The commercial independence of the South is certainly an object greatly to be desired. Is it possible to advance it more effectually, than by the concerted action of the whole South?

* * * * * * *

"'I would be wanting in the frankness and candor due to this august assemblage, if I did not plainly declare the opinions which we entertain in South Carolina. We have no confidence in any paper guarantees—neither do we believe that any measures of restriction, or retaliation, within the present Union, will avail. But with equal frankness, we declare, that when we propose a Conference, we do so with the full understanding, that we are but one of the States in that Conference, entitled, like all the others, to express our opinions, but willing to respect and abide by the united judgment of the whole. If our pace be too fast for some, we are content to walk slower; our earnest wish is, that all may keep together. We cannot consent to stand still, but would gladly make common cause with all. We are far from expecting or desiring to dictate or lead.'

"Is the proposition then, as explained by the Commissioner, any thing more than a request for a consultation among the Southern States, in order that whatever action may be deemed necessary in the present emergency, may be united in by all the States? Ought there to be two opinions as to the duty of Virginia? Ought she not to take her proper position in that consultation; and exercise her controlling influence in preserving the integrity of the Union, and securing the just and equal rights of the South? Suppose a meeting of the Southern States shall take place without Virginia? Will there not be more danger to the Union, than if she were present?

"We desire to present another consideration which, to our minds, should not be without its weight in leading us to a correct judgment upon this question. Great hope has been excited in some Southern minds, from recent demonstrations, which have taken place in the Northern States, and we are assured that the conservative element now at work there will do much towards restoring peace and harmony to the country. How can these conservative men operate with effect, when their opponents point to the failure of the proposition for the South to meet in consultation, and shall argue from that failure, either weakness, fear, or indifference. We believe that nothing will present so potent a barrier to the wave of Fanaticism which is surging over the North, as the exhibition of a *firm, united, and determined purpose*, upon the part of the South, to have 'equality in the Union, or independence out of it.' We must disabuse the mind of the North of the impression, which designing and dangerous partisans have created upon it, that the South is the embodiment of that charity which 'beareth all things, believeth all things, hopeth all things, endureth all things.'.

"We are not disposed to abandon the Union, nor to adopt such measures as must necessarily alienate still farther the North and South, and widen the breach which now so unhappily exists, between them, without another appeal to our Northern brethren, and another effort to bring back the Union to the condition of equality and fraternity, in which the framers left it. For this purpose we desire the Southern Conference to consider all questions of adjustment, and among others, the one submitted by our present able and patriotic Chief Magistrate, for a Convention of all the States of the Union. If the Union be worth saving, or can be saved, surely no effort on our part should be spared for that purpose. If it cannot be saved, at least let us have the consolation of knowing that its destruction has been accomplished without our aid, and in despite of our most earnest and determined efforts to preserve it, through all time, as a monument of the wisdom and patriotism of the Heroes and Sages of the Revolution.

"But we are not without safe precedent in this matter. Our Revolutionary Sires have taught us, not only what is our right, but our duty, in this crisis of our affairs. The Colonies sent their delegates to the first Continental Congress, because they had each causes of complaint against the Mother Country, to which they acknowledged their allegiance to be due, and desired to make common cause with the others, in order to obtain a redress of their several grievances. Their object was, not to produce a separation from the Government of Great Britain, nor to secure their independence. In the declaration made by the second Continental Congress, setting forth the causes and necessity of their taking up arms, they say, 'we mean not to dissolve that union which has so long and so happily subsisted between us, and which we sincerely wish to see restored. * * * * * * We have not raised armies with ambitious designs of separating from Great Britain, and establishing independent States.' These professions (says an able writer) of a desire for a reconciliation with the Mother Country, on terms consistent with their constitutional rights, which were so emphatically made at this time, both by the General Congress and the several Colonial Assemblies, were commonly regarded in England as nothing more than the trite, conventional language of diplomacy, and were treated as '*hypocritical and treacherous.*'

"We have the united voice of American history, and the concurrent testimony of Washington, Jefferson, and Madison, that the cry of disunion raised at that day, against those who firmly demanded their constitutional rights from the parental government, and resolved 'to die freemen rather than live slaves,' was unfounded and unjust. The cry of disunion raised now against those who seek now, by means of the proposed Conference, to secure the constitutional rights of the South, and thus to save the Union, is not less unfounded and absurd."

We have given this report almost entire, because we consider it an able and eloquent demonstration of the "Conference Scheme," and its advantages. We cannot add anything to it, so we leave it, well assured that its arguments are irrefutable.

Can any lover of the Union, or the South, refuse to respond to this call? Surely, they will not refuse to protect themselves and all near and dear to them. To save the Union, the South must be united. Divided it can do nothing. Union will give strength and dignity to its proceedings.

Let us, then, join hands—act unitedly—insist upon our rights, and maintain them at all risks—and be men and freemen indeed. Let all the great political parties unite in this measure.

It will involve no sacrifice of principles; it is a solemn duty that they owe to the South and to the Union. But it is argued, that there is a risk to run in meeting in Convention. The distinguished and talented Commissioner from South Carolina to the State of Virginia, in his address to the General Assembly of that State, on the 19th of January, 1860, thus speaks of this:

"Unquestionably there is risk; but that risk is from the perseverance of our enemies in the wrong. If they do right all will be well. Must we then accept the alternative of unconditional submission, because there is a risk of revolution? Was there ever a prize to be attained without risk? It is the law of God that everything valuable must be attained by effort. 'In the sweat of thy face shalt thou eat bread:' and this sentence is inwrought in all human possessions. Free institutions are among the most valuable of these, and they can only be maintained by constant and untiring effort.

'Oh Freedom, thou art *not* as poets dream,
A fair young girl with light and delicate limbs,
And wavy tresses gushing from her cap.
A bearded man,
Armed to the teeth, art thou; one mailed hand
Grasps the broad shield; and one the sword;
Thy brow
Glorious in beauty, though it be scarred
With tokens of old wars.' "

We leave this part of our subject, sincerely hoping that the States of the South will respond favorably to the invitation of South Carolina, and unite with her in devising means for their common defence, and the preservation of this Great Republic. But should all peaceable measures be in vain. Should the North continue to oppress us, and scorn our appeals and warnings,—then, we say, let the South withdraw and defend herself.

Should the storm ever burst, and the land be bathed in blood, let the South maintain her independence at all risks—even though her land should be laid waste; her homes destroyed; her sons and daughters slaughtered. We say, let her defend herself, even if it should come to this. She may be destroyed—utterly blotted away from amongst the nations of the earth—but her honor will be vindicated in the struggle; and she will prove that she was born to be immortal in the history of the good and great; and with her will perish the liberty of the world.

We have finished our work, and we must bid our readers *adieu*. What we have written, we have written in a spirit of kindness and love for the Union, as our fathers made it. We love all portions of it, and would see equal justice done to all. If it can honorably be avoided, we would not, for any consideration, see "one single star dimmed, or one stripe effaced" in its "banner of glory."—We would see it ever as it has been, for almost a century, the beacon-light of liberty—the home of the exiled and the oppressed.

Oh! that we could point out to our blind and misguided brethren at the North, the folly the and danger of their course; that we could bring them back to kneel at the altar where our fathers worshipped in the days of yore. We trust that the Divine Ruler who has prospered us for so long will bring all this to pass.

We trust that our humble efforts may not be in vain—but that they may help to calm the storm of Fanaticism now ready to burst upon us.

We know that Conservatism exists at the North; but alas! it is in a hopeless minority. Every day we are in receipt of the news of "Union Meetings" and "Conservative Speeches," which show that there are those at the North who sympathize with us and love the Union.

But these are not sufficient. The South must have action—legislative action at the North; her rights must be acknowledged and protected; the Constitution must be enforced, or the Union must be dissolved.

But, in leaving our readers, we beg to express the hope, that peace and tranquillity may soon be restored to us.

Then will we again have a Union of free and equal sovereign States. A Union of Freemen; then we will have such a Union as our Fathers made for us, and the prayer of every true American heart will go up to Heaven.

"ESTO PERPETUA."

Price of this Work, $10 per 100 Copies.

www.ingramcontent.com/pod-product-compliance
Lightning Source LLC
LaVergne TN
LVHW011122110826
845150LV00008B/2223

* 9 7 8 1 4 1 8 1 9 5 1 8 2 *